Kirkburn, North Humberside: an early Norman font whose motifs almost defy explanation. Pevsner calls it 'a barbaric jumble'. Nevertheless, a bishop holding a crozier is clearly recognisable. Compare with Avebury, page 12.

CHURCH FONTS

Norman Pounds

Shire Publications Ltd

CONTENTS

Published in 1995 by Shire Publications Ltd, Cromwell House, Church Street, Princes Risborough, Buckinghamshire HP27 9AA, UK.

Printed in Great Britain by CIT Printing Services, Press Buildings, Merlins Bridge, Haverfordwest, Dyfed SA61 1XF.

British Library Cataloguing in Publication Data. A catalogue record for this book is available from the British Library.

Cover: *The font at Luppitt, Devon (see also page 14).*

ACKNOWLEDGEMENTS
Photographs are acknowledged as follows: courtesy of B. T. Batsford, pages 1, 13 (top right and bottom), 14 (top), 30 (left); Cadbury Lamb, cover, pages 2 (both), 4, 6 (top and bottom), 8 (both), 11 (bottom right), 12 (bottom, both), 13 (top left), 14 (bottom), 17 (left), 19, 23 (bottom, both), 25 (both), 26 (both), 27 (all), 28, 29, 30 (centre), 31. All other photographs are supplied by the author.

Derbyshire: (left) at Youlgreave a thirteenth-century font with restrained decoration and a curious spout or stoup, underneath which is carved a salamander, symbolising the virtue of the righteous man. The single motif on the bowl relates it to (right) the thirteenth-century font at Ashbourne. There are a few other fonts with similar motifs in the 'Ashbourne' group.

An early medieval painting of the baptism of Christ in the church of Asinou, Cyprus.

BAPTISMAL FONTS

Towards the west end of the nave of almost every parish church in Britain and close to the main entrance stands a baptismal font. It is a welcoming symbol, not only to every visitor to the church today, but also to every new member of the Anglican communion who has been baptised in it over a period of many centuries. There have been some ten thousand ecclesiastical parishes, both rural and urban, in England and Wales, but considerably fewer in Scotland. Most still retain a parish church and, within it, a baptismal font, for the font was, with the cemetery which enclosed the church, a mark of parochial status, distinguishing the church from a chapel of ease or private chapel. In the past one could assume that almost every parishioner had been baptised at this font while still only a few days or weeks old, given a name, admitted to the community of the parish, and, in the eyes of the theologians, absolved from the stain of original sin. In medieval Britain and for a long while after the Reformation, baptism was held to be essential if the child was to escape damnation. So urgent and necessary was baptism seen to

be that that it was permitted at home if the child was too sickly to be brought to the church. And, if no priest could be summoned, the rite could legitimately be performed by a lay person, even by the midwife, who for this reason was required to be licensed by her diocesan bishop.

Human life is punctuated by moments when a person changes from one status or occupation to another. Puberty and marriage are such occasions, but the most significant of these 'rites of passage' were those which marked the beginning and the end of life. Both were distinguished by rituals which symbolised them and at the same time made them memorable to all who participated. Baptism is a rite of passage by which a child or convert is admitted to the fellowship of the Christian church.

BAPTISM IN THE EARLY AND MEDIEVAL CHURCH

From the earliest days of the church baptism was the rite by which the Christian laid aside the past and was freed from the stain of sin. Christ had been baptised by John the Baptist in the waters of Jordan,

3

and the early church tried, whenever possible, to re-enact this ritual. Early converts were, of course, adults. Whether they were actually submerged during the ritual or, as is more likely, had water poured over them as they stood in the river, is not altogether clear. More often than not there was no river nearby, and baptism took place in the bath which was a feature of every fashionable Roman house. The usual practice after the recognition of Christianity by Constantine in AD 312 was to construct a baptistery for this purpose.

In structure and arrangement the baptistery derived from the domestic bath-house. Eventually it came to be a square, round or, most often, octagonal building, in the midst of which was a tank or small bath in which the ceremony took place. Baptisteries were to be found at one time in most cathedral cities, for in the early church it was the bishop who performed the rite. Such baptisteries long continued in use in southern Europe, and the structures themselves, sometimes in ruins or converted to other uses, are still to be seen in many French and Italian cities. In England there is evidence for there having been a baptistery at Canterbury, but nothing of it survives.

The situation in Britain was radically different from that in southern Europe. Towns were few and very small and the population was predominantly rural. It would have been difficult for converts, especially the very young, to make the journey to their cathedral city. It was far better to take the rite to them in their parish churches up and down the land. The season for baptism in the early church had been around Easter or Whitsuntide, but in Britain it early became the practice to baptise a child as soon as possible after birth. As Britain gradually became christianised it was mainly the young who were brought to church for baptism, and this in turn reinforced the tendency to hold the ceremony amid the local communities. A large and pretentious baptistery on the Italian model would have been inconceivable, though it is possible that some humbler structure, perhaps adjoining a spring or holy well, may have been used.

Infant baptism in the local church became and has since remained the normal practice in the English church. This was reflected in the form which came to be adopted for the font. The font is essentially a bowl sufficiently large for a child to be placed within it, though total immersion seems never to have been practised. The bowl of early fonts was round and usually large, up to a metre in diameter and 0.75 metre deep. It was fitted with a drain and some kind of a plug. The water used had been sanctified and was allowed to remain in the font for prolonged periods. At intervals, however, it was allowed to drain away into the subsoil of the church. The practice was unhygienic, but so was much else in the everyday life of early Britain. Sometimes the water was stolen and used for superstitious purposes, so that from the thirteenth century fonts were fitted with locked covers.

Deerhurst, Gloucestershire: this must be one of the oldest surviving fonts in Britain. The spiral decoration covering most of the bowl has been dated to the later Anglo-Saxon period. Below it is an interlace. The base has been much mutilated. The font was rescued from a farmyard in the mid-nineteenth century.

4

Polstead, Suffolk: a highly unusual late medieval octagonal font, built of brick in an area lacking in suitable stone. Imported stone would have been very expensive

Many early fonts were of wood and resembled a kind of barrel, but the church disapproved of the use of wood, possibly because it tended to rot and thus to contaminate the water held in it. Nevertheless, a finely carved font of oak remains in use in the church of Marks Tey in Essex. However, stone came into general use from an early date. A very few fonts, such as that at St Martin's, Canterbury, were built of masonry, but this would have allowed the water to escape through the mortar lines and so the bowls of almost all surviving fonts have each been carved from a single block of stone. This might be granite or other igneous rock, marble or, as in the great majority, a free-cutting limestone. The best and most widely used material came from the limestone belt which lies across England from Dorset to Yorkshire. In East Anglia many of the finest fonts have been carved from clunch, a relatively hard form of chalk which lends itself to delicate carving. A number of fonts are of the bluish Purbeck 'marble' from Dorset. They are all relatively shallow, as this attractive stone occurs only in thin beds. Purbeck fonts are to be found over much of south-eastern England, but generally only where they could be transported by water from the Dorset coast. Another distinctive group of fonts, also found near the coast of south-eastern England, was carved from a black marble found near Tournai in Belgium. A far greater number of these fonts is to be found in north-western Europe. Their decoration shows them to have been of the twelfth century, and their close similarities make it probable that they were all made close to the quarry from which the stone was taken and were then despatched by boat to their purchasers.

A small group of about a dozen twelfth-century fonts was made from lead and cast in moulds. There would appear to have been a foundry near Bristol and perhaps others in London and elsewhere.

Whatever the material used, with the exception of lead, there was the danger that water would soak into it and perhaps damage the stonework. For this reason most fonts were lined with a thin sheet of lead, which often overlapped the rim. Post-Reformation fonts usually lacked this lead lin-

St Martin, Canterbury, Kent: a twelfth-century font with geometrical decoration. It is built of masonry; the mortar lines are clearly visible. The pattern of interlinked circles was common at this time.

Left: *Winchester Cathedral, Hampshire: a twelfth-century font of black Tournai marble with scenes of the miracles of St Nicholas. About ten such fonts survive in England and many more in continental Europe. They are all markedly similar in design and decoration and were probably carved close to the marble quarry.*

Right: *Wareham, Dorset: one of the few fonts made of lead; hexagonal in plan, with two bays of arcading on each face. One figure is identifiable as St Peter; the rest are probably apostles. The bowl is set on a masonry support of Purbeck marble.*

ing, firstly because an impervious material such as marble was often used, and secondly because it ceased to be the practice to hold water in the font.

The Reformation made little difference to the theological position. Baptism continued to be required by canon law, and the state lent its support to the insistence of the church. Churchwardens regularly reported to the church courts, over which the archdeacon usually presided in the name of the bishop, that

Gloucester Cathedral: font from St James, Lancaut, 1130-40. There are six late twelfth-century leaden fonts in Gloucestershire sufficiently alike to suggest the use of the same moulds. The workshop may have been in Bristol or Gloucester.

Padstow, Cornwall: a beautiful fifteenth-century piece carved in the hard Cataclew stone which occurs in the cliffs nearby. Half-figures of angels are at the corners and saints in the niches. The neighbouring parish of St Merryn has an almost identical font of the same material. They must be by the same craftsman.

certain named parents had not brought their child to be baptised.

Not until the eighteenth century, with the decline in the jurisdiction of the church courts and the coming of a more tolerant attitude, were the rigours of canon law relaxed. Most of those who had failed to have their children baptised into the established church were either recusant, that is Roman Catholic, or nonconformist. The latter included Baptists, who practised adult baptism, and Quakers.

Baptism was no less a civil and a social occasion than a religious one. Except on the rare occasions of a private baptism, it was a public ceremony. It was a gathering of the families of both parents, and to these were added the 'godsib' or godparents. Their theological role was to ensure the proper upbringing of the child and to attend to its spiritual welfare should the real parents die prematurely. On the social side they extended the kindred group, bringing persons from outside the family into that group. This was important because there was a degree of friendship and mutuality within kinship, and the more friends a person had within the closed local community the fewer were the potential enemies to trouble him or her. At baptism the child became a person with a name, a member of both the Christian and the civil community of the parish, and was burdened with obligations to both.

In 1538 Thomas Cromwell, Henry VIII's chief minister, ordered a record of baptisms to be kept in each parish. The ordinance met with a degree of resistance, and there are few parishes which possess a complete record from that date. The injunction was repeated by Elizabeth I, who furthermore prescribed that it should be kept in a book of parchment leaves. Most parishes can show registers, kept with varying degrees of care, from about this time. They record the date of baptism, the name given to the child and the names of both parents. Twins and triplets were usually recorded as such. The baptism of illegitimate children sometimes cost the minister some pangs of conscience. Canon law required that they should be baptised like any other, but occasionally the minister allowed his indignation to overflow on to the pages of the register, expressing his feelings in the strongest terms.

A christening was a memorable occasion, made more so if it was followed, as it often was, by a feast. Before modern times people were all too aware of the passage of the seasons, but of the succession of the years they had little record. Few had any certain knowledge of their own age. When, for example, a young man was left a barony or an estate by the death of his father, it was of vital importance to establish his age. If he was under eighteen the king or his overlord might manage and profit from his possessions until he reached the age of maturity. An enquiry, known as an *inquisitio post mortem*, was held. Witnesses were called, and time and again a witness would claim to have been present at the baptism of the young man; by linking this with some known event, a date would then be established. It was assumed that birth could have been only a few days earlier.

Ilam, Staffordshire: possibly the work of an amateur, as distinct from the professional carver.

EARLY MEDIEVAL FONTS

Although one can trace a straightforward line of evolution from the simple fonts of the eleventh century to the elaborately carved masterpieces of the pre-Reformation era, there are many which belong to no particular genre. They reflect the extravagances or the incompetence of local craftsmen or the poverty of a parish, compelled to make do with any piece of stone that was available and could be hollowed out to form a bowl.

The earliest fonts were rounded and shaped like tubs. Then they began to be cut from roughly rectangular blocks of stone, thus providing four panels which could be further carved and decorated. Both shapes, round and square, continued to be used throughout the twelfth and thirteenth centuries, but their decoration became increasingly elaborate. In the fourteenth and fifteenth centuries an octagonal (occasionally hexagonal) form came into fashion and remained the most favoured shape until the Reformation. Although these forms came to prevail generally, it must be remembered that most fonts were not made in any central workshop or according to accepted patterns.

They were carved by local craftsmen whose ideas were sometimes old-fashioned and often idiosyncratic. The localisms are most conspicuous in the decoration and the iconography or symbolism carved on the fonts. One cannot say whether a group of closely similar fonts emanated from a single workshop or was the product of an itinerant craftsman with his repertoire of designs, or even whether they were made by someone who had carried in his mind's eye the pattern of a distant font which had attracted his attention. There was a strong element of imitation in the production of medieval fonts.

Altarnun, Cornwall: one of a group of closely similar fonts. There is documentary evidence that one of them belongs to the early thirteenth century. They were all probably the work of a single craftsman.

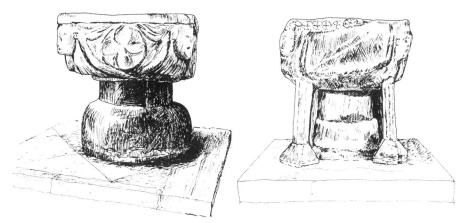

(Left) A typical Altarnun-type font at Warbstow, Cornwall. (Right) A crude imitation at Tintagel, Cornwall. The octagonal corner pillars are a much later addition.

A curious example is to be found in north Cornwall. Here, and in neighbouring parts of Devon, are a dozen or so fonts of the so-called Altarnun type. They are large and square at the top; most are carved in granite, and all have face masks at the corners. On each side of the bowl, which is rounded, there is a stylised flower partially encircled by a snake-like creature with a single body and two opposed heads. The massive bowl is supported on a short thick pedestal. At Tintagel, on the coast, is a comparable font, made not of granite but of a distinctive local igneous rock, a dolerite known locally as 'greenstone'. The block of stone used is irregular; its carved detail is amateur in the extreme, but its motifs represent a crude imitation of those found on an Altarnun-type bowl. It is a reasonable assumption that the Tintagel font was the work of a local man who, in his unskilled fashion, tried to reproduce the work of a professional craftsman working elsewhere. One of the delights of studying fonts is the discovery of such examples of the ways in which medieval people lived and worked.

The following are the most important and widespread of the types of font to be found in parish churches today. They are described in their historical sequence so that their evolution can be traced.

Tub fonts. Amongst the oldest surviving fonts are the rounded, tub-shaped type, each cut from a single block of stone. One of the crudest is that at Morwenstow in north Cornwall. Most have little or no decoration, beyond a chevron or cable moulding, which could serve to date them, but they probably belong to the later eleventh or early twelfth century. Within a relatively short period the tub font evolved into the pedestal font. First a 'waist' appeared, encircled, girdle-like, by a simple moulding. Then the lower part was gradually narrowed until it had become a stem or pedestal.

Morwenstow, Cornwall: a very early tub font, cut from a single block of dark 'elvan', with slightly constricted 'waist' and cable decoration. It is difficult to date but is probably of the eleventh or early twelfth century.

9

Shobdon, Herefordshire: bowl and stem are ill-matched in this twelfth-century font. The style of the lions passant around the stem resembles that on the bowls of the Bodmin type and is almost certainly of the twelfth century and of the Herefordshire school of sculpture. Compare with Eardisley, page 13. The lead lining protrudes above the damaged rim.

Square fonts. Of similarly early date are square fonts, each cut from a single large block of stone. Their rectangular panels invited decoration. At its simplest this might be no more than a shallow arcade. Sometimes each face was divided into smaller panels, each with a figure or motif. The font at Burnham Deepdale, Nor-

folk, is decorated with scenes depicting the Labours of the Months. That at Winchester Cathedral portrays the story of St Nicholas. Some of these fonts are almost cube-shaped, thus providing four large panels for relief carving. That at Lenton, in Nottinghamshire, exhibits a rich array of sculpture. The fonts of Tournai marble display both religious themes and legendary beasts. Most of the Purbeck marble fonts are of a similar shape, since the rock occurs only in shallow beds.

The stone used had often been cut from relatively shallow beds, and the fonts in consequence were too low for convenience. They had to be lifted above the floor in order to allow an infant to be placed in them. This was done by raising them on a shaft, which might be up to a metre in height. For the very large square fonts a single central pedestal often proved inadequate and had to be supplemented by corner shafts. Sometimes these corner shafts were clumsy and inartistic. In order to make them more appealing they were sometimes closely clustered, even attached to one another, and decorated. It also became the practice, certainly before the end of the twelfth century, to mount the pedestal and corner shafts on bases. The analogy with the pillars in the arcade of a church is close, and the shafts themselves came to have carved bases and capitals. The font thus became tripartite, consisting of the bowl, the pedestal and shafts, and the base. Each part was made separately and the font was assembled in the church, the parts being mortared or leaded together. In consequence, all three parts might today be of different dates and made of different materials. A medieval bowl is often found supported by a modern pedestal and base, or a modern bowl resting on a shaft of much earlier date. This tripartite design was retained for most fonts throughout the later middle ages and has been repeated in many of more recent date.

Tickencote, Leicestershire: a late Norman font with an arcade and above it rather stylised trailing vegetation. At the corners are face masks.

Burnham Deepdale, Norfolk: a late twelfth-century font showing four of the Labours of the Months: (from right to left) January, February, March, April. Detail: September, threshing with a flail.

Lenton, Nottinghamshire: font of the twelfth century cut from a cuboid block of limestone. Its sides are covered with a maze of incised scenes, amid which it is impossible to see any underlying plan.

Fulbeck, Lincolnshire: the splendour of this Transitional font is, perhaps, the result of re-tooling but it is a fine example of a Lincolnshire style; see also Deeping St James, page 17.

11

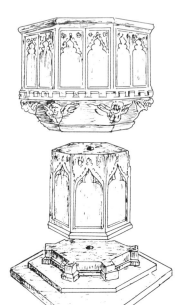

Left: *Sculthorpe, Norfolk: late twelfth-century rectangular font. The panel on the right depicts the adoration of the Magi.*

Right: *Construction of a typical late medieval font, showing the drain.*

DECORATION ON EARLY FONTS

Most early fonts were relatively plain, their ornamentation consisting of little more than a cable, chevron or star moulding. In the course of time decoration became more complex. On the one hand it came to embrace symbols and imagery appropriate to the rite being carried out; on the other, decoration became increasingly architectural and included miniature arcades and tracery such as one would find in the fabric of the church itself. Be-

Left: *Avebury, Wiltshire: a twelfth-century font with rounded intersecting arches below a frieze with a bishop (holding a crozier) and a dragon.*

Right: *Eaton Bray, Bedfordshire: for a period in the thirteenth century 'stiff-leaf' foliage was used to decorate the font bowl, reflecting contemporary developments in architecture.*

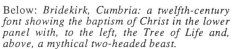

Below: *Bridekirk, Cumbria: a twelfth-century font showing the baptism of Christ in the lower panel with, to the left, the Tree of Life and, above, a mythical two-headed beast.*

Above: *Weston Turville, Buckinghamshire: this 'chalice' pattern font of the early thirteenth century shows the stylised Romanesque leaf decoration merging into 'stiff-leaf' (see Eaton Bray, page 12). The base is in the shape of an inverted cushion capital. This type is found especially around Aylesbury.*

fore the fourteenth century, however, most decorative motifs fall into the following five groups:

The human head. This is a recurring motif in early medieval art. Such functional devices as corbels were often carved to show a human face, and the head was a common feature on early fonts not only in Britain but throughout western Europe. It was sometimes carved on tub fonts, but the corners of a square font were ideal for them. A number of examples are illustrated in this book. In the south-west of England there is a very large group of fonts which exhibits this motif. Not all are of the early middle ages; the motif continued to be used up to the Reforma-

Left: *Eardisley, Herefordshire: one of the finest surviving twelfth-century fonts. Its carving is of the Kilpeck school, because some motifs are identical to those in the finely decorated Norman church at Kilpeck in the same county.*

tion. It is difficult to discover a meaning for this recurring symbol; in the end it probably had little. But to the early Celts the head, as the seat of wisdom, had great significance. Many of them had been head-hunters. But we cannot know whether in the Christian period the head was seen as a witness to the sacrament or as a representative of the heavenly host (many later examples are shown with wings).

Legend and folklore. A number of fonts show incidents from the lives of saints, in

Brookland, Kent: one of a small group of leaden fonts. They were cast in sections in moulds and then joined with molten lead. The lower panels depict a favourite medieval motif, the Labours of the Months. The upper panels show the signs of the zodiac.

particular of the saint to whom the church in which the font is found is dedicated. Perhaps because of his association with children, the story of St Nicholas appears on some, for example at Brighton and in Winchester Cathedral. More often than not, these motifs form a jumble that can be extremely difficult to unravel, as at Luppitt in Devon and Lenton near Nottingham. A few fonts show the Seven Virtues, or at least a selection of them, triumphing over the corresponding vices. Southrop in Gloucestershire and Stanton Fitzwarren in Wiltshire are particularly attractive examples. At Brookland in Kent and Burnham Deepdale in Norfolk the symbolic Labours of the Months are shown.

Another decorative feature found on many early fonts is the Tree of Life. This

Hook Norton, Oxfordshire: a tub font with very primitive decoration, including a Tree of Life.

Luppitt, Devon: an early twelfth-century font with face masks at the corners and extraordinarily primitive carving (see cover picture).

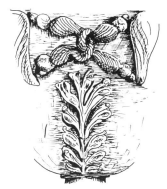

A common rope-like motif with the Tree of Life below. This decoration is common to the Bodmin fonts.

Drawing of the thirteenth-century font at Bodmin, Cornwall, c.1790. From the notebook of Samuel Lysons in the British Library. This is the finest of a group of Cornish fonts, all of which display similar motifs.

motif is both biblical and pagan and is taken to typify the new life in Christ into which the child is introduced by the rite of baptism. The tree assumes many forms, all of them highly stylised.

Pagan symbolism. When the early fonts were being carved, elements of paganism were still present in the beliefs of ordinary people. It is difficult to reconcile some of the symbols seen on many fonts,

especially those in the West Country, with any aspect of Christian theology. Take for example those fonts which make up the Bodmin group. They are large, square-topped, with deep bowls rounded on the outside, and are supported by a central pillar and four corner shafts. At their corners are male human heads, while over the bowl itself is a profusion of mythical creatures. These include reptiles with fangs and long tails; cat-like creatures, often in pairs facing one another; and, most mysterious of all, rope-like mouldings worked into knots and patterns. What these meant to the people who sculpted them we cannot know; it is possible that they had already lost any precise meaning

(Left) St Stephen's-by-Saltash; (right) Maker (originally at St Merryn), both in Cornwall. These are fonts of the Bodmin type and show the primitive decoration common to all of them. They probably represent the work of a single craftsman or workshop.

The development of font styles.

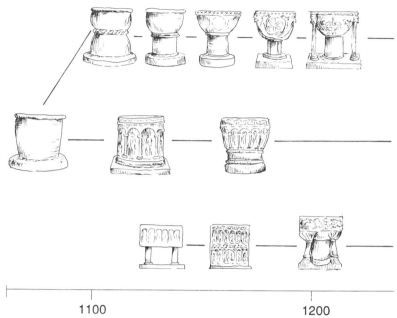

1100　　　　　　　　　　　　　1200

and had degenerated into an acceptable form of decoration. St Bernard of Clairvaux, writing in the middle of the twelfth century, objected to his monks being distracted by such art, which, he clearly thought, was

Cathedral of St Woolos, Newport, Gwent: a twelfth-century font, with foliate heads (the 'green man') at the corners. This device, common in the twelfth- and thirteenth-century sculpture, is very rare in fonts.

devoid of meaning. A reptilian figure also appears on other groups of fonts, notably those of the Altarnun type. A pagan motif which does sometimes have some meaning, however, is the 'green man'. He is not often found on fonts, but in East Anglia he appears as a 'supporter', carved against the pedestal, and at St Woolos in Newport, Gwent, he appears as a 'foliate head' with greenery spewing out of his mouth.

St Peter's-by-the-Castle, Cambridge: twelfth-century font with double-tailed mermaids at the corners; compare St Woolos, Newport.

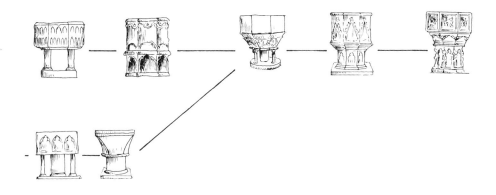

1300	1400

Geometrical decoration. Many early fonts are decorated with geometrical or architectural patterns. There may be an arcade of rounded arches, as at Egloshayle in Cornwall; the arches are interlaced, as at St Martin's Canterbury. Sometimes there is an irregular pattern of concentric circles, stars or flower-like motifs; sometimes there is an interlace or plait. At Preston in Suffolk there is a comprehensive display of such figures.

Southrop, Gloucestershire: a beautifully carved thirteenth-century font, with cusped niches containing figures both military and ecclesiastical.

Deeping St James, Lincolnshire: a very fine late twelfth-century font with arcade decoration. There are a number of such fonts in Lincolnshire, suggesting a common craftsman or workshop.

17

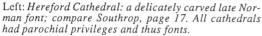

Left: *Hereford Cathedral: a delicately carved late Norman font; compare Southrop, page 17. All cathedrals had parochial privileges and thus fonts.*

Right: *Rendcomb, Gloucestershire: similar to Southrop and Hereford Cathedral but a generation or more earlier. Note the round arches of the arcade.*

Naturalistic decoration. The thirteenth century, when Early English Gothic merged into Decorated, was marked by a more tasteful and less haphazard application of decoration. This was the time when naturalistic leaf decoration appeared, as well as tracery in the windows and attached and clustered columns in the arcades of churches great and small. It would be surprising if this burgeoning had not

Left: *Barnack, Cambridgeshire: this delightful thirteenth-century font is lavishly decorated with stiff-leaf foliage. The fine-grained local limestone lends itself to this kind of decoration.*

Right: *Bibury, Gloucestershire: early thirteenth-century Romanesque (Norman) cable moulding survives in the corner pillars. The font is otherwise of Decorated Gothic style of the mid to late thirteenth century.*

Brailes, Warwickshire: above a plain pedestal the panels of the bowl are filled with examples of the curvilinear tracery of thirteenth-century windows.

been reflected in the design of fonts. Free-flowing motifs replaced the rigidity of geometrical decoration. The fonts at Barnack in Cambridgeshire and in Peterborough Cathedral luxuriate in the wealth of foliage which envelops them.

At the same time architectural features were absorbed into font design. Pedestals were made to resemble the columns of a nave arcade. The panels of the bowl were decked out with tracery. There can be few Gothic windows with tracery more complex than that which appears on the font at Brailes in Warwickshire. By the thirteenth century fonts in general retained their traditional forms, whether square or round, with or without pedestals and corner shafts, but they were shaped more gracefully and decorated with greater skill and sophistication.

LATE MEDIEVAL FONTS

The fourteenth and fifteenth centuries were marked by a growing uniformity in the design of fonts, as they were also by an increasing rigidity in church architecture generally. Local styles, idiosyncratic forms and free-flowing decoration gave way to tripartite fonts of octagonal design. There was an increasing uniformity also in the use of materials. Gone were the black marbles of the twelfth century and the colourful shelly marbles of the thirteenth. Instead, almost every font was of free-working limestone. Some, like those of Hadleigh and Rattlesden in Suffolk and Fishlake in South Yorkshire are works of very great beauty, but most represent the competent products of workshops located mainly in London and the chief provincial cities. Circular and square fonts were out. The octagon was in, with very occasionally the hexagon. Octagonal bowls were mounted on octagonal pedestals, and these in turn on octagonal bases. The three pieces were delivered to the church for assembly. All that was required was a firm floor with a soakaway for the drain, and lime mortar to fix the parts together.

Now and again one finds some echo of an earlier style: a cable or a chevron moulding, a face mask or even a base inherited from an earlier font. Sometimes an older font was hacked about, its corners cut off to make it conform with the newest fashion. One can see such a clumsy piece of vandalism at March in Cambridgeshire. Instances are probably quite numerous, but in many cases the artifice was disguised by the skill of the craftsman. Overall, many of the churches which were rebuilt in the Perpendicular style in the fifteenth century threw out their earlier fonts and installed one of more fashionable and contemporary design.

Despite their superficial similarity, octagonal fonts came in many patterns, varying with the stone used, the workshop in which they were made, and the amount which the parish was prepared to pay. Simplest and presumably cheapest was

20

Badingham, Suffolk: a Seven Sacraments font of the fifteenth century. The central panel shows the sacrament of baptism. An unusual feature is the panels carved in the stem showing some of the prophets. Detail: the sacrament of Extreme Unction.

the octagonal bowl with its panels left plain, as at Wootton Wawen in Warwickshire. On the underside of the bowl two or three roll-mouldings linked it with the pedestal, also plain, which stood on a moulded base. The majority of octagonal fonts were, however, decorated. It was as if the parish ordered the standard model but specified the nature and degree of decoration that was to be applied to it. There might even have been the medieval equivalent of a pattern book from which the customer was free to choose. Most popular amongst the forms of decoration available were:

Trefoil and quatrefoil decoration. Each panel was carved with a single repetitive design. There might be from one to four trefoils or quatrefoils to each panel. Much depended on its size and shape. Or the panels, especially if they were high in

relation to their width, might be treated as if they were traceried Gothic windows, as at Offley in Hertfordshire and Patrington in North Humberside. At Hitchin, Hertfordshire, the panels became cusped canopies raised above niches, the figures which were conceived as occupying the latter being set against the pedestal. These designs were not symbolic; they had no significance beyond relieving the monotony of an empty space. These fonts differ only in detail, in the height of the bowl, in the mouldings which enclosed the panels and in the number, size and detail of the mouldings on the underside of the bowl.

Seven Sacraments fonts. These were amongst the most sophisticated fonts created during the middle ages. There had been earlier fonts which portrayed the baptism of Christ; that at St Nicholas,

21

Sloley, Norfolk: Seven Sacraments font of eight panels. The central panel shows the sacrament of penance. Details: (below) the rite of baptism, (bottom) of holy matrimony.

Brighton, shows him standing in the Jordan while John poured water over him. But the Sacraments fonts of the fifteenth century went much farther than this. Not only did they represent the sacrament of baptism as it was practised at this time, they also showed the other six sacraments on the remaining panels and filled in the last with a crucifixion or other religious 'picture'. Representations were realistic and, within the limits set by the material used, accurate. Such sculpture called for a homogeneous and relatively soft limestone. Such a stone was clunch or Totternhoe stone, which was to be found only in eastern England. It is here that almost all the existing sacraments fonts are to be found; forty-two are known to exist, forty of them in Norfolk and Suffolk. There is one at Farningham in Kent and a curious outlier at Nettlecombe in western Somerset. How, one wonders, did the design get there?

22

Left: *Binham Priory, Norfolk: a Seven Sacraments font. Many monastic houses, notably those of the Benedictine and Augustinian orders, had parochial rights and thus baptismal fonts.*

Right: *Nettlecombe, Somerset: a Seven Sacraments font (after Paley), a long way from all the others of this type in East Anglia.*

Other motifs. The panels of an octagonal font were an open invitation to the sculptor, who often used his skills to the uttermost. Amongst the more common motifs were the four evangelists and the four Fathers of the Church (probably Saints Ambrose, Augustine of Hippo, Jerome and Gregory the Great), alternating with some other device. There were stylised floral designs and shields, occasionally carved with the armorial bearings of a patron or benefactor, or, more often, left plain to be coloured. Such an heraldic font is to be found at Holt in Clwyd. Many fonts, if not all, originally had some colouring, and not infrequently some trace of paint can still be found. The panels were picked out with reds, greens and blues. There may have been gilding, and flesh-coloured paint was probably used on human features. The font at Haddenham in Cambridgeshire still retains a good deal of its original colouring.

Snape, Suffolk: eight figures encircle the base and figures fill the panels of the bowl, each holding part of a long scroll. But one panel (see centre left) shows God, holding in his lap Christ crucified, flanked by angels aloft.

Above: *Stoke-by-Nayland, Suffolk: on the bowl are the symbols of the evangelists and four other figures. The steps on which the font stands are made to form seats, beneath the arms of two local families, Tendring and Howard, which presumably paid for the font.*

Decorated pedestals. In the more elaborate of late medieval fonts the underside of the bowl, the pedestal and even the base were highly decorated. Decoration consisted as a general rule of complex mouldings which reduced the diameter of the bowl to that of the pedestal. These were sometimes ornamented with foliage or winged angels. The panels of the pedestal were carved to look like a traceried window, and even cut into niches, as at West Drayton in Middlesex. These were originally occupied by figures cut in rather shallow relief, as at Kessingland and Cratfield in Suffolk and East Dereham in Norfolk. The corner mouldings between the panels were sometimes enlarged into

figures or grotesques. These might be animals – usually lions – in an almost upright or 'sejant' position, as at Lound in Suffolk, or less frequently human figures or the wild or green man, as at Happisburgh and Acle in Norfolk. The green man was traditionally one who had escaped the restraints and demands of civilised society and typified a kind of licentious freedom. His appearance as a kind of 'supporter' on the pedestals of a few late medieval fonts is possibly one of the last survivals of pagan imagery in the church. In some earlier fonts the lower edge of the bowl had been scalloped. This kind of decoration was developed in a few late medieval fonts into swags of pendant foliage. In the best of these later fonts the bowl, pedestal and base were knit together by their decoration into a unified artistic whole.

Haddenham, Cambridgeshire: fifteenth-century font retaining some of the original colouring. Rosettes and angels appear in the panels of the bowl and four griffins support the stem.

24

Left: *Blythburgh, Suffolk: this is one of the very few fonts that are securely dated. It was made in 1449. It has, however, been severely mutilated. The panels, which may have contained representations of the Seven Sacraments, have been smoothed away with a chisel.*
Right: *Chipping Campden, Gloucestershire: half of an early thirteenth-century font protrudes from an interior wall of the church, where it is occasionally used as a flower holder.*

THE REFORMATION AND AFTER

Churchwardens' accounts, which form the only significant record of parochial income and expenditure during the later middle ages and early modern times, occasionally note the purchase or repair of a font. They also record, though fortunately less frequently, their damage and destruction. The sacraments became very much less important in protestant Britain, but that of baptism continued to be required within the established church as well as in most nonconformist churches, and fonts continued to be an essential item in the furnishings of those of the Anglican communion. The records of visitations made by bishops or their deputies to the parishes within their dioceses not infrequently note the condition of the font. But this did not prevent their mutilation, sometimes on a savage scale. We find part of a font cut away to make room for the construction of a family pew for an influential parishioner; we find a churchwarden who tried to achieve a kind of posthumous fame by having his name engraved – artistically, it must be conceded – on the rim of the font; and we have fonts from which all 'superstitious' symbols and representations have been chiselled away. The

Seven Sacraments fonts suffered severely in this way: that at Blythburgh in Suffolk has had its carving chiselled off, and very few of those which have survived are intact. Lastly, fonts have suffered from the mindless vandalism of all ages which knocks off heads and gouges initials into their surface. More understandably, many whose surface had become rough with age were recut, often in a way which destroyed many of their original features.

Many fonts which had become damaged or dated were merely turned out of the church and replaced with new ones. Some found a resting place in the churchyard, the vestry or the tower. Others were incorporated into later church building; at Chipping Campden in Gloucestershire half of a font protrudes from an interior wall, where it is used as a flower basket. Some disappeared into private gardens or even farmyards, from which a few have in recent times been rescued. Many a newly built church has been able to acquire a redundant font from an older church or even to retrieve one from a farmyard, but many hundreds must have been lost for ever. A fragment of a twelfth-century Tournai marble font has, for example,

Harrow-on-the-Hill, Middlesex. When this Norman font was restored to the church in 1846 (after being saved from destruction previously by a parishioner who kept it in her garden) the restorers broke off the original rim and kept the fragments as keepsakes!

come to rest in the Christchurch museum in Ipswich, and the present writer once found a tiny piece of a font of a familiar early pattern in the vestry of a West Country church.

POST-REFORMATION FONTS

From a fifth to a quarter of existing fonts were made after the Reformation. They conformed to no particular pattern. Few were made in the later sixteenth century or during the period of Puritan domination in the seventeenth century. The sacrament itself, if not exactly neglected, was treated with little respect, and the frequency with which the bishops ordered that it should not be performed in 'basins' suggests that the font itself may have ceased to be used. The few fonts that were set up during this period conformed with traditional patterns, with the addition of contemporary decoration, like the font in Great St Mary's, Cambridge, which is

dated to 1632. Then, with fresh church building in the later seventeenth century and during the eighteenth, a number of new fonts were made. These were mostly of classical design. Their bowls were small, their pedestals finely turned, and their water-holding capacity slight. Such fonts are to be seen at Blyth in Nottinghamshire and in the Wren churches of London.

This reflected a change in the administration of the rite. The child was no longer partially immersed but instead was sprinkled with water, a practice which has continued to the present. This obviated the need for a large and deep bowl. As water was no longer held in the bowl the need for a lead lining also disappeared. The number of such fonts is not great, and most are to be found in newly built or

Tideswell, Derbyshire: this late medieval font was found by a vicar in a rubbish heap where it had languished since the eighteenth century. It had been used as a paint pot when the church was painted.

Grosvenor Chapel, London: a number of fonts of this delicate pattern were made in the late seventeenth and early eighteenth centuries. Many are to be found in the City of London, where churches were rebuilt after the Great Fire of 1666.

Left: *Exeter Cathedral, Devon: another datable font, made for the christening of Henrietta (born 21st July 1644), youngest daughter of Charles I.*

Lichfield Cathedral, Staffordshire: a richly carved Victorian font of about 1860, which makes use of a variety of coloured stones.

Boston, Lincolnshire: this extravagantly decorated font was designed by E. W. Pugin, son of the great A. W. N. Pugin. It follows a medieval pattern.

rebuilt churches like those on some great estates and in the City of London.

In the nineteenth century there was a complete change in fashion. The Oxford Movement brought with it a return to Gothic forms in architecture and ornamentation. At the same time many new churches were built primarily to serve the needs of a growing urban population. With scarcely an exception, their fonts were flamboyantly Gothic and attempted to perpetuate the medieval tradition. They are, however, readily distinguishable: they use exotic materials; their decoration is often excessive; they have no lead lining and there is no evidence for the staples which in older fonts had served to secure the font cover to the rim.

FONT COVERS

Canon law required the water held in the font to be renewed each week but, as some visitation records show, it was often held very much longer than this. It is evidence for the long survival of pagan and superstitious practices that the water was not infrequently stolen and used in sorcery and other rites. In an effort to stop this, an Archbishop of Canterbury ordered fonts to be covered. In 1287 Bishop Quivil of Exeter went farther, ordering that the cover should be securely locked into place. Other bishops followed, and into modern times it was normal for fonts to be locked. Indeed, one of the most frequent complaints made in the course of diocesan visitations of parish churches was that the font was inadequately secured.

Haddon Hall, Derbyshire: formerly in the neighbouring parish church and probably of the twelfth century, this font was very roughly cut from a single block of stone. Damage caused by staples securing a cover can be seen on the left. The stem and base are probably later.

The usual method was to cover the entire top of the font with a wooden disc fastened in place by means of a metal bar which was locked to staples driven into the rim. Inevitably the staples did irreparable damage. Portions of the rim were sometimes broken away, or the iron staple rusted, expanded and cracked the stone. In many fonts one finds a piece of new and sometimes different stone dovetailed into the rim. In many more there is either a damaged rim or a fragment of metal left from the staple. Such telltale signs are irrefutable evidence of a pre-Reformation date.

Many parishes were not content with a simple wooden cover. Instead, they installed towering tabernacles of wood with elaborate tracery and pinnacles. These were very heavy, and most were fitted with a pulley and tackle for lifting them. The cover at St Gregory, Sudbury, Suffolk, is typical of these complex wooden structures, but the one at Ufford, also in Suffolk, is probably the largest. It is so high that it reaches into the roof. As it is too tall to be lifted to uncover the font, the lower part has been made to retract over the middle and upper parts – one of the most ingenious examples of medieval engineering. In some churches a modern cover has been made to cover the font. It usually fits only loosely and cannot be secured. At best these are only competent examples of the joiner's craft.

The need to protect the sacred water from the malicious and the superstitious sometimes led parishioners to enclose their font within a kind of free-standing cupboard, with a door which could be locked and opened only when the font was in use. Such protected fonts are few, but examples can be seen at Thaxted in Essex and St Botolph's, Cambridge. They are indeed so well protected that one cannot examine the fonts without obtaining the key!

Left: *Beverley Minster, North Humberside: a very large font of about 1530, of Frosterley marble (a north country equivalent of Purbeck) decorated with a simple arcade. The cover is a magnificent piece from the seventeenth century.*

Above: *St Botolph, Cambridge: an enclosed font so carefully protected that it is almost impossible to examine the font itself, which is plain, late medieval and octagonal. According to the churchwardens' accounts, the casing dates from 1637.*

Left: *St Gregory, Sudbury: a late fourteenth-century octagonal font with one of the finest and most architectural of late medieval covers in Britain.*

FURTHER READING

Bond, Francis. *Fonts and Font Covers*. Oxford University Press, 1908; second edition, Waterstone, 1985.

Clarke, K.M. 'The Baptismal Fonts of Devon', *Report and Transactions of the Devonshire Association*, volumes 45-54, 1913-22.

Cox, J.C., and Harvey, A. *English Church Furniture*. Methuen, 1907; reprinted, EP Publishing, 1973.

Davies, J.G. *The Architectural Setting of Baptism*. London, 1962.

Drake, C.S. 'The Distribution of Tournai Fonts', *Antiquaries Journal*, volume 73, 1993.

Druce, G.C. 'Lead Fonts in England', *Journal of the British Archaeological Association*, volume 39, 1934.

Eden, C.H. *Black Tournai Fonts in England*. E. Stock, London, 1909.

Fisher, J.D.C. 'Christian Initiation: Baptism in the Medieval West', *Alcuin Club Collections*, volume 47, 1965.

Fryer, A.C. 'Leaden Fonts', *Archaeological Journal*, volume 57.

Fryer, A.C. 'On Fonts with Representations of the Seven Sacraments', *Archaeological Journal*, volume 59, 1902.

Fryer, A.C. 'Gloucestershire Fonts', *Transactions of the Bristol and Gloucestershire Archaeological Society*, volumes 36-46, 1913-24.

Paley, F.A. *Illustrations of Baptismal Fonts*. J. Van Voorst, London, 1844.

Tyrrell-Green, E. *Baptismal Fonts*. SPCK, London, 1928.

Wall, J.C. *Porches and Fonts*. W. Gardner, Darton & Company, London, 1912.

Brant Broughton, Lincolnshire: a simple fifteenth-century octagonal font with a Victorian cover of traditional design. The lower part is hinged and opens out so that the font can be used.

SELECT GAZETTEER

Every Anglican parish church contains a font. Up to a quarter are modern, especially those in urban churches, but the great majority of rural churches contain medieval fonts.

A number of local studies of fonts have been published, most of them in the relevant county archaeological journals. County museums and collections often contain drawings and photographs of fonts. In the following lists fonts are grouped by form, material or decoration.

Fonts with primitive or pagan sculpture
Buckinghamshire: Stone.
Cornwall: all fonts in the Bodmin group (see below).
Cumbria: Bridekirk.
Devon: Luppitt.
Dorset: Melbury Bubb.
Hereford and Worcester: Castle Frome, Chaddesley Corbett, Eardisley, Shobdon.
Northamptonshire: Harpole.
Nottinghamshire: Lenton.
Shropshire: Holdgate.
Warwickshire: Curdworth.
Wiltshire: Avebury.
Yorkshire, North: North Grimston.

Lead fonts
Avon: Siston.
Buckinghamshire: Penn.
Derbyshire: Ashover.
Dorset: Wareham.
Gloucestershire: Aston Ingham, Down Hatherley, Frampton-on-Severn, Gloucester Cathedral (fonts from Lancaut and Tidenham), Haresfield, Oxenhall, Sandhurst, Slimbridge.
Hampshire: Tangley.
Hereford and Worcester: Burghill.
Humberside, South: Barnetby-le-Wold.
Kent: Brookland, Eythorne, Lower Halstow, Wychling.
Norfolk: Brundall.
Oxfordshire: Childrey, Dorchester, Long Wittenham, Warborough, Woolstone.
Surrey: Walton-on-the-Hill.
Sussex, West: Edburton, Greatham, Parham, Pyecombe.

Tournai marble fonts
Hampshire: East Meon, St Mary Bourne, Southampton (St Michael), Winchester Cathedral.

Humberside, South: Thornton Curtis.
Lincolnshire: Lincoln Cathedral.
Suffolk: Ipswich Christchurch Museum (fragment), Ipswich (St Peter).

Aylesbury-type fonts
Bedfordshire: Dunstable, Houghton Regis, Linslade.
Buckinghamshire: Aylesbury, Bledlow, Chearsley, Chenies, Great Kimble, Great Missenden, Haddenham, Little Missenden, Monks Risborough, Pitstone, Weston Turville.

Bodmin-type fonts
Cornwall: Bodmin, Kea, Luxulyan, Maker, St Austell, St Goran (or Gorran), St Newlyn East, South Hill, Veryan.

Altarnun-type fonts
Cornwall: Altarnun, Callington, Jacobstow, Landrake, Laneast, Launceston (St Thomas), Lawhitton, Lezant, Tideford, Warbstow.
Devon: Ashwater, Bratton Clovelly.

Seven Sacraments fonts
Kent: Farningham.
Norfolk: Alderford, Binham, Brooke, Burgh-next-Aylsham, Cley, Earsham, East Dereham, Gayton Thorpe, Gorleston, Great Witchingham, Gresham, Little Walsingham, Loddon, Marsham, Martham, Norwich Cathedral, Salle, Seething, Sloley, South Creake, Walsoken, Wendling, West Lynn.
Somerset: Nettlecombe.
Suffolk: Badingham, Cratfield, Denston, Laxfield, Melton, Monk Soham, Southwold, Westhall, Weston, Woodbridge.